Punctuation Without Tears

PUNCTUATE CONFIDENTLY
— IN MINUTES!

Dominic Selwood

ILLUSTRATIONS BY
Delia Johnson

CORAX

Published in Great Britain by
CORAX
London

Visit our author website
www.dominicselwood.com

British Library Cataloguing in Publication Data.
A catalogue record for this book is available from
the British Library.

ISBN 978-0-9926332-9-5

Typeset by Corax in Bembo Book MT Pro and Gill Sans MT

Yesterday Mr. Hall wrote that the printer's proof-reader was improving my punctuation for me, & I telegraphed orders to have him shot without giving him time to pray.

MARK TWAIN
Letter to William Dean Howells regarding the proofs of
A Connecticut Yankee at the Court of King Arthur
21 August 1889

Do you know any body who can stop — I mean point — commas & so forth — for I am I fear a sad hand at your punctuation.

LORD BYRON
Letter to John Murray regarding the proofs of
The Giaour
26 August 1813

I have to thank you for punctuating the sheets before sending them to me as I found the task very puzzling — and besides I consider your mode of punctuation a great deal mo[re] correct and rational than my own.

CHARLOTTE BRONTË
Letter to Smith, Elder & Co regarding the proofs of
Jane Eyre
24 September 1847

"Essential reading for anyone wanting to impress with their CV"
JAMES INNES — *Bestselling careers author, UK and USA*

"Selwood has done the impossible: he has produced a short and funny book on punctuation. Whether you are eight or eighty, you will want this indispensable guide beside you, as a reminder of all those rules you have been told, but have long since forgotten."
DR JAMES W P CAMPBELL — *Bestselling author and Fellow of Queens' College, University of Cambridge, UK*

"This is everything I want from a book about punctuation: it made me laugh and cheer. Our children are being taught the odious Spelling, Punctuation, and Grammar with rigid rules and no creativity. We all should be embracing punctuation with Selwood's passion."
HENRIETTA MCMICKING — *Award-Winning BBC Producer, UK*

"Dominic Selwood demystifies the — often arcane — rules of modern punctuation. Written in a lively tone, with the focus firmly on the essentials, he'll have you telling your commas from your semicolons in no time! Highly recommended to anyone seeking to write with accuracy and verve."
DR LEVI ROACH — *Lecturer and Award-Winning Author Department of History, University of Exeter. UK*

"Students and teachers dread SPAG (spelling, punctuation and grammar), yet these are essential for clear written communication. This book is not only entertaining in itself, but neatly lays out the standard conventions which make for good writing, without pedantry."
THE REVD DR SIMON THORN — *Teacher, Winchester College, UK*

"As a professor for 40 years, most of them at Harvard and now at Oxford, I fancy myself an expert on punctuation. At the same time, I have lived in fear of violating fundamental and inviolable truths, while ruthlessly correcting the punctuation of students and colleagues. What a relief to have read Dominic Selwood's delightful little book on this subject! The same will be true for every reader of this book. He or she will punctuate better and feel more confident in doing so."
PROFESSOR ROBERT ECCLES — *Said Business School, University of Oxford, UK*

"A short, pithy, yet comprehensive guide on punctuation. I can see this guide becoming used widely. And deservedly. I would recommend this book to anyone wishing to cut through the complexities and arcane rules of punctuation. Period!"
GEORGE ROBERTS — *Teacher, Hoylake, UK*

"Of course punctuation matters. It matters to you! Were one to have read, carefully, Dominic Selwood's excellent book finding so much as one grammatical or punctuation error, the author would gratefully refund your full purchase price and buy his former tutor, me, a beer. So, do read very carefully!"

REV JOHN MAXWELL KERR — *Former Professor, Research Fellow in Physics and Chemistry, and Chaplain, University of Oxford, UK, and College of William and Mary, USA*

"As an editor and writer of fiction and nonfiction, I get all worked up over punctuation. Dominic Selwood helped me to see a new way through the rules and assumptions and also how to relax."

NANCY BILYEAU — Bestselling *author, Journalist, Editor, USA*

About the Author

Dominic Selwood is a columnist for Britain's *Daily Telegraph* newspaper. He writes occasionally for *The Spectator* — Britain's oldest periodical — and other newspapers and magazines. He is the author of a number of bestselling novels and history books, and appears as a commentator on television and radio. He has a doctorate from the University of Oxford.

He tweets at:
@DominicSelwood

Contents

CHAPTER I

Punctuation is About You

For centuries, people have tried to turn punctuation into a science with dozens of rigid rules. But it's actually much more fluid than that. The reality is that there are almost no unbreakable rules.

I offer one guiding principle for effective punctuation:

Do whatever makes your writing easiest to understand

That may sound too good to be true, but it makes sense when you remember that the purpose of punctuation is to help readers understand what you write.

My second piece of advice is:

Punctuate according to the context

A children's picture book and an instruction manual on making a thermonuclear bomb will use very different writing styles. It's natural that their punctuation will be different, too.

So, from the outset, get into your mind that punctuation is flexible and varied.

If you flip through some older books, another thing you'll notice is that punctuation has changed a lot over time.

I'm not going to go into the whole fascinating history of punctuation (or "pointing" or "stopping", as it used to be called), but it's helpful to know that, for thousands of years, writing was just chunks of letters jammed together, with no spaces and no punctuation. Something like this:

> Scrunchingwordstogetherwasnormalingreekand
> latinandlookedsomethinglikethisasyoucanseeit
> takesabitofefforttoreadandmostpeopletoday
> wouldnotwanttoreadawholebookwrittenlikethis

As time went on, writers and copyists tried to make writing easier to understand. They put gaps in between words, and added little marks to make the text more intelligible. They soon came up with dozens of signs — like interpuncts, diastoles, trigons, and diples — and they used them in imaginative ways. The problem was everyone did it differently, leaving readers to struggle with a baffling variety of punctuation systems.

Once printing took off in the late 1400s, publishers started to standardize the chaos. After a lot of trial and error, they settled on using periods (full stops), commas, colons, and the other marks we know today.

However, even though we've been using a standard set of punctuation marks for several centuries, there have always been fashions in how they're used.

To see what I mean, pick up a random selection of books from the last five hundred years, and you'll see just how tastes in punctuation have changed — often wildly.

*For thousands of years, writing was just chunks of letters
jammed together, with no spaces and no punctuation*

For instance, this is how Shakespeare's *First Folio* of
1623 printed the famous "To be or not to be" speech.
To be kind, I've updated the spelling, which was also
pretty different back then:

> To be, or not to be, that is the Question :
> Whether 'tis Nobler in the mind to suffer
> The Slings and Arrows of outrageous Fortune,'
> Or to take Arms against a Sea of troubles,
> And by opposing end them : to die, to sleep
> No more ; and by a sleep, to say we end
> The Heartache, and the thousand Natural shocks
> That Flesh is heir to?

In all honesty, no one would print the speech like this today. It's all random capitals, haphazard punctuation marks, and rambling structure. A publisher today would ask for it to be crisp, unambiguous, and readable. Perhaps something like this:

> To be, or not to be? That is the question.
> Whether 'tis nobler in the mind to suffer the
> slings and arrows of outrageous fortune, or to
> take arms against a sea of troubles, and — by
> opposing — end them. To die, to sleep …
> no more. And by a sleep to say we end the
> heartache, and the thousand natural shocks that
> flesh is heir to.

If you think you'd do it a different way, that's absolutely fine. In fact, that's brilliant. It's exactly how you should be thinking. There's no "right way". Punctuation is personal and demands choices.

So, remember:

Punctuation is about individual style

There are very few absolute rules in this book. Punctuation is largely down to you — just like the words, images, sounds, and rhythms you choose in your writing.

I'm not being trendy or radical in saying this. As long

ago as 1762 a leading expert on punctuation wrote pretty much the same thing:

> Few precise rules can be given, which will hold without exception in all cases; but much must be left to the judgement and taste of the writer.

So, here's another piece of guidance:

Be creative with your punctuation

By that I mean: choose it carefully. Allow it to help you express what you want to say. Use it to get the mood of the writing across. But don't go mad. If you make the punctuation too striking, it'll become a distraction, and that's a writing disaster. Think of punctuation as the unseen scaffolding that holds the text in shape. It needs to stay in a supporting role, and should never find itself in the spotlight.

That is, of course, unless you want the punctuation to take a star turn. For example, the American writer E E Cummings (or e e cummings) shot to fame because of his outrageous punctuation. Here's his 1954 poem called *!blac*:

!blac
k
agains
t

(whi)

te sky
?t
rees whic
h fr

om droppe

d
,
le
af

a:;go

e
s wh
IrlI
n

·g

His poetry is weird, and mad, and fabulous. But it's not exactly mainstream. And — this is the point — Cummings was well aware his maverick punctuation was a statement. He was shouting to the world, "Look at me! My writing is art!"

If you want to be the next E E Cummings, that's great. It's probably time someone did it again. But if you want to write clear and intelligible English that'll get you nods of approval from people who immediately see you know what you're doing, then read on.

CHAPTER 2

Three Golden Rules

Traditional punctuation guides are filled with dozens of baffling rules that have built up over the years.

I'm not a fan of that approach. I'm going to offer three simple principles:

Be clear
Be creative
Be consistent

If you follow these three principles, you'll be punctuating effortlessly and confidently in no time.

CHAPTER 3

Period or Full Stop

This is the mother of all punctuation marks. If you were asked to produce a piece of writing with only one punctuation mark, you should choose this one. This small glyph has the power — all by itself — to bring order out of chaos.

In the U.S. it's called a period. In Britain it's called a full stop. Over the years it's also been known as a point, a full point, and a stop. I'm going to call it a period.

WHAT DOES IT DO?

The period has two uses. (1) Ending a sentence. (2) Abbreviations.

ENDING A SENTENCE

Everyone knows this one. You put a period at the end of a sentence:

> Gandalf thumped the furball hard. He hated hobbits.

It couldn't be simpler. Periods end sentences.

Gandalf thumped the furball hard. He hated hobbits.

What might perhaps be a little trickier, though, is knowing exactly where to end a sentence.

Traditional grammar books say things like, "a sentence is a set of words which is complete in itself" or "a sentence is a completed thought". I don't find this type of definition especially useful or practical.

Hopefully the following will help.

Keep Sentences Short

If you pick up a novel from the 1800s — say, something by Charles Dickens — you'll see that in his day it was fine for a sentence to ramble on and on and on, often for a whole paragraph. Here's the opening of his great novel A *Tale of Two Cities*:

> It was the best of times, it was the worst of times, it was the age of wisdom, it was the age of foolishness, it was the epoch of belief, it was the epoch of incredulity, it was the season of Light, it was the season of Darkness, it was the spring of hope, it was the winter of despair, we had everything before us, we had nothing before us, we were all going direct to Heaven, we were all going direct the other way — in short, the period was so far like the present period, that some of its noisiest authorities insisted on its being received, for good or for evil, in the superlative degree of comparison only.

Today, a publisher would tear his or her hair out if anyone sent that in. Fashions in writing have changed dramatically. Readers today expect punchy, short sentences that make the writing easy to digest. Something like this:

> It was the best of times. It was the worst of times. It was the age of wisdom. It was the age of foolishness.

Or, if you're feeling a bit daring (see Chapter 6 on semicolons):

> It was the best of times; it was the worst of times. It was the age of wisdom; it was the age of foolishness.

The point is that we're now in the twenty-first century. Don't be a Dickens. Keep sentences short. The practical reason for this is simple: shorter sentences are far clearer to read and understand. So if you find a sentence droning on for several lines, find a way to break it up.

You don't need a verb

You may have heard that a sentence must have a verb. Strictly speaking — if you want to be the grammar police — that's absolutely true. The shortest possible full sentence is just two words. Something like, "Dracula awoke" or "Jesus wept" (which is famous as the shortest sentence in the Bible).

However, while it's technically true that a sentence needs at least two words — a subject and a verb — this is now totally irrelevant, and you can safely forget about it. Why? Because no one insists you write in whole sentences any more. The world has moved on. Honestly.

In the previous paragraph I wrote two one-word sentences. Twenty years ago it would've raised eyebrows. These days it's fine. People now use sentences of just one or two words all the time.

One reason is that it's how people speak. One- or two-word sentences often reflect the natural rhythms of modern thought and speech:

> The minion raised the saw. "This isn't going to hurt. Much."

It feels natural to write it like that, because that's how it's spoken.

Another reason to use very short sentences occasionally is that they can create a terrific effect. Like this. Or this. You'll see lots of writers doing it to inject drama:

Vector loaded the Squid Launcher. He licked his
lips with anticipation. He would show them. All
of them. Tonight.

So, really, when it comes to sentences, keep them
short and feeling natural. As long as you do that, you
have infinite freedom. When you're done with each
chunk, just add a period at the end. Period.

ABBREVIATIONS

A while ago, people put a period at the end of a word
to show it had been abbreviated. This was especially
true of the commonest Latin abbreviations:

Anno Domini	A.D.
post meridiem	p.m.
exempli gratia	e.g.
id est	i.e.
et cetera	etc.

It was also very common with English words that
were frequently abbreviated:

Professor	Prof.
General	Gen.
United Kingdom	U.K.
January	Jan.
Monday	Mon.

The period in these words indicates that at least one letter is missing at exactly the place where the period is placed. So the period in "Jan." shows that a number of letters — in this case "uary" — have been sliced off.

For this reason, many people — and I am one — will not put a period after Mr, Mrs, Dr, and other similar words that are contractions rather than abbreviations. In these cases the missing letters are from the middle of the word rather than the end. For me, if someone wrote "Dr." it would indicate that letters are missing after the letter "r", which is not the case.

However, unless you're writing for a very traditional publication, you don't really need to put periods into abbreviations at all any more. Most publishers today try to make the page look less fussy, so they've ditched these periods and just write "pm", "eg", "Prof", and so on. This is especially true in business writing, where you almost never see periods for abbreviations any more.

One major exception, and it's just one of those quirky traditions, is that many publishers still use periods for "the U.S.". There's no real reason why. It's just a tradition.

In the end, when it comes to abbreviations, unless

your publisher has a house style, it's up to you. Just be consistent.

SPACES AFTER A PERIOD

When printing began, centuries ago, printers used one, two, three, or even four spaces at the end of a sentence. By the early twentieth century, most publishers agreed that one space was best. However, when typewriters became widely available in the late 1800s, people using them started putting two spaces after a period. This is because typewriters print equally spaced letters, which leave so many gaps that it's easier to see the end of a sentence if there are two spaces.

That was then. Today the rule is clear. Typographers, style guides, and experts all say the same thing. Use one space. If you are sending your manuscript to a publisher, he or she will not want to see two spaces. And if you are producing the work yourself, your word processor will use modern typefaces that are proportionately spaced, and the text will look far more professional with just one space.

CHAPTER 4

Comma

After the period, the next most vital punctuation mark is the comma. Used well, the simple comma is the key to making your writing crystal clear.

Commas are also the punctuation mark that says the most about you as a writer. The comma offers you many options, and the decisions you make with it tell the reader a lot about the way you think.

WHAT DOES IT DO?

The comma has four uses. (1) Breaking up sentences. (2) Lists. (3) Dividing off speech. (4) Some traditional uses.

BREAKING UP SENTENCES

Over the years, people have laid down a thousand and one rigid rules for how to use commas. Many of them are mind-bendingly technical and don't mean anything unless you're a professor of grammar.

The good news is that, unless you're a professor of grammar, you really don't need to know any of them.

The "Pause Rule"

Here's a simple, liberating reality:

Ignore the old rules

I'm going to replace them with just one very simple one:

**Use a comma when you pause or change
the pitch of your voice**

I'm going to call this the "Pause Rule".

Basically, if you want to know where to put a comma, read the sentence to yourself slowly. Wherever you pause or change the pitch of your voice, add a comma.

Read the following sentence aloud, slowly, and with expression. Read it as if you're reading a bedtime story to a child. Do it a couple of times, until you feel you're really putting some feeling into it:

> Snow White who could not bear Sneezy's poor hygiene any longer went to look for her axe.

You almost certainly paused in two places and changed the pitch of your voice at those points. I'm going to put commas at those places:

> Snow White, who could not bear Sneezy's poor hygiene any longer, went to look for her axe.

It's as easy as that. A grammarian will use a lot of technical terms to explain what you've just done. Happily, you don't need to. All you have to know is that you've just punctuated the sentence correctly.

Now, try this one:

> Feeling homesick Cthulhu snuggled his tentacles up under the duvet.

You probably paused once:

> Feeling homesick, Cthulhu snuggled his tentacles
> up under the duvet.

Again, you've put the comma where the grammarians say you should.

The Pause Rule is a quick hack that covers ninety-nine per cent of the formal rules on commas. That said, there are a couple of simple situations you can learn to recognize in order to make it all even easier.

Joining sentences

When you join two sentences with "and", "but", or any other linking word, the sentence reads better if you add a comma before the "and", "but", or the other linking word. The Pause Rule works fine to identify these situations, but linked sentences happen so often you might want to learn to spot them anyway.

For example, look at this:

> He spent a restless night in his coffin. He
> dreamed sporadically of his hamster.

We can join them with "and":

> He spent a restless night in his coffin and he
> dreamed sporadically of his hamster.

However, we can make it all even clearer for the reader by adding a comma:

> He spent a restless night in his coffin, and he
> dreamed sporadically of his hamster.

This comma helps the reader separate out the two different ideas in the sentence. When they read it, they'll know to add a short pause before the "and".

It should be obvious that I'm talking about instances when you use "and" to join two sentences. You plainly wouldn't put a comma before an "and" when it's being used in a simple list like, "I hate garlic and crucifixes".

He spent a restless night in his coffin, and he dreamed sporadically of his hamster.

"Comma off" clauses

This is another occasion when the Pause Rule works fine, but you might want to learn to recognize the structure because it occurs so often. Once you begin seeing it everywhere, you'll start adding commas naturally.

It happens when you drop words into a sentence as an introduction, explanation, or aside. Grammar books call these "clauses". (There are other types of clause, too, but they're not relevant here.)

The acid test for one of these clauses is simple. Can you remove the words completely, but still be left with a sentence that makes perfect sense. For example:

> The deranged woodsman, armed only with a
> spoon, glared furiously at the hedgehog.

Now, take away the words "armed only with a spoon" and you can see that you're left with a sentence that still makes perfect sense. It has slightly less information in it, but it flows like a sentence, and reads just fine:

> The deranged woodsman glared furiously at the
> hedgehog.

The Pause Rule works here, too. When you read the

sentence aloud, you naturally put little breaks where the commas are. But these clauses occur in writing all the time, so it's worth learning to recognize them.

LISTS

You need commas in lists of things:

> The werewolf loved howling, gorging, yodelling, and his Ladyshave.

It's a very straightforward principle. You put a comma after each item in a list.

The same is true of lists made up of descriptive words (adjectives and adverbs):

> The bouncy, exuberant, inquisitive, engaging, exotic, psychotic werewolf.

The rule is the same for all lists: use commas to divide them up.

The Serial Comma

At some stage in your life, you'll probably have been told — perhaps very sternly — to omit the last comma in a list of three or more, like this:

> The books that made Snow White happiest were:
> *Ant and Bee*, *The Tale of Mrs Tiggy-Winkle* and
> *The Necronomicon*.

But, I bet you've seen people disobeying the rule:

> Prince Charming asked the palace orchestra to
> play all his favourites at the grand ball: a waltz, a
> minuet, and *The Ace of Spades*.

Exasperated teachers may have put a red line through
your work if you ever tried to add this last comma.

However — be strong! — this extra comma has been
used for centuries. It's absolutely fine to add it in. It
even has a name. It's called the serial comma, series
comma, Harvard comma, or Oxford comma. You can
guess from the fact it's linked to Harvard and Oxford
that it really is fine to use it. Thousands of writers and
publishers use it all the time. I've used it throughout
this book.

Usually, people put in this extra comma as a matter of
personal choice and style. But watch out. Sometimes
it's absolutely necessary for clarity. Look at this:

> Drago gave the chocolate crucifixes to his
> brothers, Vlad and Wadim.

If you think about this sentence, it's ambiguous.
It could mean that Drago handed out three lots of

chocolate crucifixes: one lot to his brothers, one lot to Vlad, and one lot to Wadim.

Or, it could mean that Drago handed out two lots of chocolate crucifixes: one lot to Vlad and one lot to Wadim, who are both his brothers.

If the writer meant that he handed out three bundles, then a serial comma will magically take away the ambiguity:

> Drago gave the chocolate crucifixes to his
> brothers, Vlad, and Wadim.

On the other hand, if he only gave out two lots, then a colon would actually be much clearer (Chapter 5 will explain why):

> Drago gave the chocolate crucifixes to his
> brothers: Vlad and Wadim.

The serial comma is also useful when you have things that need to go together:

> "Let's spend some time with each other,"
> the dementor suggested. "We can enjoy tea,
> strawberries and cream, and sucking out joy."

Here, "strawberries and cream" is a thing, like "bed and breakfast" or "country and western". Putting in the serial comma helps to keep the sense.

DIVIDING OFF SPEECH

You need a comma with speech. This is also covered by the Pause Rule, but it's easy to remember, so I'll mention it.

You ought to put a comma before or after quotation marks when someone is speaking. It's traditional, and readers expect to see one:

> The goblin smiled nastily, "Who ironed my pyjamas?"

> "Bring my favourite duck," Darth Vader ordered, striding into the steamy bathroom.

As you can tell when you read the sentences, you pause a little at the comma.

See Chapter 12 for where to put the comma when you use quotation marks.

"Bring my favourite duck," Darth Vader ordered, striding into the steamy bathroom.

SOME TRADITIONAL USES

You should be aware that some introductory words and phrases are traditionally followed by a comma.

However, Therefore, Moreover

If you start a sentence with "however", "therefore", "moreover", or similar words, it's normal to put a comma after it:

> However, now the octopus came to think of it, she had already given her fingerprints.

Therefore, with a heavy sigh, the warlock put his grimoire away.

Moreover, she remembered that eating frogs gave her hiccups.

Dates and Times

It's also traditional to put a comma after an opening date or time:

In 1487, two German priests wrote *The Hammer of the Witches*: a handy guide for Inquisitors when torturing Satan's spawn.

At 3.00 pm, she went down to the dungeon and checked the fridge for canapés.

You don't have to put in this comma, but you'll see it a lot.

At 3.00 pm, she went down to the dungeon and checked the fridge for canapés.

A HORROR: THE COMMA SPLICE

A comma sin to avoid at all costs is the comma splice.

A comma splice happens when you try to join two sentences with a comma.

> Goldilocks swung the nunchuk, she liked its weight.

> The woodsman hated bunnies, he hated them with a Luciferian mania.

It's not good style, and readers know it's wrong. Each of these examples is two complete sentences. They therefore need a period (or a semicolon, if you're feeling inspired) between them.

> Goldilocks swung the nunchuk. She liked its weight.

> The woodsman hated bunnies; he hated them with a Luciferian mania.

This is, though, one of those cases where there are rare exceptions. If you're Charles Dickens, no one is going to stop you from using a comma splice. Look at the beginning of *A Tale of Two Cities* again:

> It was the best of times, it was the worst of
> times, it was the age of wisdom, it was the age of
> foolishness, it was the epoch of belief, it was the
> epoch of incredulity, it was the season of Light,
> it was the season of Darkness, it was the spring
> of hope, it was the winter of despair, we had
> everything before us, we had nothing before us,
> we were all going direct to Heaven, we were all
> going direct the other way …

This is thirteen comma splices in a row. Pretty impressive. But I wouldn't recommend trying this today.

CHAPTER 5

Colon

The colon is not used much these days, and its purpose is often misunderstood. But it's actually very simple to use, and easy to get the hang of.

WHAT DOES IT DO?

The colon has three uses. (1) Lists. (2) Quotations. (3) Explanations. In all these cases, it takes the reader firmly but caringly by the hand, and leads them to the information they're looking for.

In many cases you can also use a dash instead of a colon to give a more relaxed feel (see Chapter 9).

LISTS

The colon lets a reader know that you're starting a list:

> All sorts of things get stuck in Wookie fur: duct tape, intergalactic dust, and small mammals.

It's as simple as that.

In the past, especially in Britain, people sometimes put a hyphen or dash after the colon (:- or :–). Typographers called this combination "the dog's b–llocks", for obvious reasons. No one uses it any more. (For dashes in impolite words, see Chapter 9.)

QUOTATIONS

Colons also work for starting quotations:

> As Darth Vader's light sabre scythed through Obi-Wan Kenobi, a gentle voice drifted up from the heap of hot clothes where the mage had stood: "This will not look good on my resumé."

As with lists and explanations, the colon here is introducing the next section of the sentence.

EXPLANATIONS

When speaking, people sometimes say things like:

> It was the monk's malign incantation, i.e., his
> foul curse.

By saying "i.e." they are introducing an explanation. When writing, you can simply use a colon to do this:

> It was the monk's malign incantation: his foul
> curse.

This also goes for phrases like "that's to say", "in other words", or other phrases leading to an explanation.

You can also use a colon for broader explanations where you wouldn't use "i.e.". For example:

> Tinkerbell was angry: knife-sharpeningly angry.

> Simba's secret was out: he hated her Chihuahua.

> Santa Claus wanted just one thing for Christmas:
> revenge.

The text after the colon can be a word, a few words, or a whole sentence. But in all cases the colon guides the reader to the payoff.

COLONS AND CAPITALS

In British English you always follow a colon with a lower-case letter. In U.S. English it's different, as some U.S. publishers prefer you to put an upper-case letter after the colon if it starts a complete sentence:

Simba's secret was out: He hated her Chihuahua.

You mainly see this in quality publishing and technical writing. But don't try doing it in British English as people will think you've made an error.

CHAPTER 6

Semicolon

After a long and useful life, the semicolon is now, tragically, in the Emergency Room. Worse, some doctors are seriously debating whether or not to put a "Do Not Resuscitate" sign at the end of its bed.

As a result, it's increasingly common for people to tell you to forget the semicolon completely. However, I'm not one of them. If you're a carpenter, why would you throw away one of your tried-and-tested tools? There are jobs it was made for, and it will do them better than anything else in your toolbox.

The semicolon is the same. It evolved for certain specific purposes and, unsurprisingly, it fulfils them better than other punctuation marks. When it's needed, it delivers.

Those who say the semicolon is at death's door point to its slow decline over the last hundred years. For example, as long ago as 1939, the British writer George Orwell decided to write his novel *Coming up for Air* without any semicolons at all. He explained:

> I had decided … that the semicolon is an
> unnecessary stop and that I would write my next
> book without one.

In 2005, the American writer Kurt Vonnegut went further:

> First rule: Do not use semicolons. They are
> transvestite hermaphrodites representing
> absolutely nothing. All they do is show you've
> been to college.

I love Kurt Vonnegut. He's one of my all-time favourite writers, but I don't agree with him on this.

Even though the semicolon is not as popular as it once was, it has definite uses, and when you need it, there's no other punctuation mark that can take its place.

WHAT DOES IT DO?

The semicolon has two uses. (1) Weak period. (2) Complex lists.

WEAK PERIOD

Look at this:

> The prince loved beautiful song birds. He ate
> them every day.

It's perfectly punctuated. It follows the modern trend of using short sentences. The reader gets the point clearly. There is no ambiguity.

Now look at this.

> The prince loved beautiful song birds; he ate
> them every day.

The semicolon here has done something a little magical. It has softened the break between the two sentences. Somehow the two ideas now snuggle together a little better. And, in a nutshell, that's what the semicolon does. It allows you to link two sentences so they almost flow into each other. It's a mark of intimacy. It brings a connectivity and balance no other punctuation mark can. Using a semicolon like this has a pleasing, literary feel.

The real masters of the semicolon were the Victorians. Here's a sentence from Charles Dickens's *Bleak House*:

> Harold Skimpole loves to see the sun shine;
> loves to hear the wind blow; loves to watch the
> changing lights and shadows; loves to hear the
> birds, those choristers in Nature's great cathedral.

The repeated semicolons here make the ideas jumble together in a sort of mad stream of childish consciousness. You get the sense Harold Skimpole is a bit immature and unhinged — which it turns out he is. Dickens was a genius.

Of course, you would never get away with a sentence like that now. A publisher would be scratching away furiously with a red pen on your manuscript. But there's no reason why you can't use a semicolon occasionally. It's a thing of beauty; it adds a little shimmer of fairy dust.

COMPLEX LISTS

There's one circumstance in which you absolutely need a semicolon. It doesn't have a literary feel like the above examples, but it's important for basic sentence structure. Look at this unpunctuated list:

> Harald a Viking Eggnog a Saxon Rollo a
> Norman Cheops an Egyptian Gizmo a Gremlin

If you use commas, you get this:

> Harald, a Viking, Eggnog, a Saxon, Rollo,
> a Norman, Cheops, an Egyptian, Gizmo, a
> Gremlin.

The problem is that this is still unclear. It could mean there are five people there, or perhaps ten people. Semicolons will clear it up nicely:

> Harald, a Viking; Eggnog, a Saxon; Rollo,
> a Norman; Cheops, an Egyptian; Gizmo, a
> Gremlin.

In really disorganized lists the semicolons can be even more critical:

> The larder was full of good things hot chilli
> peppers pre-packaged cubed salt cod kidney
> beans coloured pink fine icing sugar plums
> spaghetti carbonara sauce dauphinoise potatoes
> thin frozen steak chips etc

Semicolons let you be clear which words go together:

> The larder was full of good things: hot chilli;
> peppers; pre-packaged, cubed, salt cod; kidney;
> beans; coloured, pink, fine icing; sugar plums;

spaghetti carbonara; sauce dauphinoise; potatoes;
thin, frozen, steak chips; etc.

The semicolons divide up the confusing information
into neat chunks in a way you couldn't do just with
commas. They make the list instantly intelligible.

CHAPTER 7

Exclamation Mark

Exclamation marks are a lot of fun! They are popular in informal writing, e-mails, messaging, and other personal communication, where they add a sense of exuberance and excitement.

However, you need to be careful with them in more serious writing, as they draw a lot of attention to themselves, which is not always appropriate. Some people loathe them. The American writer F Scott Fitzgerald said they are like laughing at your own jokes. That's a little harsh, because the exclamation mark has its place. But do be careful. A dialogue in a novel that includes a rash of exclamation marks is not going to impress anyone. Use them sparingly.

WHAT DOES IT DO?

The exclamation mark has one main use: to mark when something is exclaimed, shouted, or surprising.

EXAMPLES

The exclamation mark is very simple to use. Just put it at the end of a sentence instead of the period:

> Danger! Minions on holiday.

> Gandalf felt the ring's demonic power course through his veins. "This," he smiled, "is fun!"

You can also use exclamation marks inside sentences. I did, earlier, when talking about the serial comma. I wrote:

> However — be strong! — this extra comma has been used for centuries.

There's nothing wrong with that, although you wouldn't do it without the dashes or some other way of separating off the phrase. It wouldn't look right if the exclamation mark was just floating freely in the middle of the sentence.

The important thing with exclamation marks is to use them carefully. They are great in informal writing like texts and e-mails, where they help to make the writing more friendly. But too many of them in a work of fiction starts to look out of control, and you should almost never use them in formal writing.

CHAPTER 8

Question Mark

The question mark should be, by far, the simplest punctuation mark. However, people sometimes find it confusing, although they needn't. Its role is very straightforward.

WHAT DOES IT DO?

The question mark has one main use: to indicate that something is a question.

EXAMPLES

If the sentence is a question, you put a question mark at the end instead of a period:

> Cthulhu wrapped his decaying tentacles tighter around the old fisherman. "Where did you put the strawberry cheesecake?"

You can also use a question mark inside a sentence:

> "Spartans!" he thundered. "Tonight we dine in … bother, what was it again? … oh, yes, I remember — hell!"

Cthulhu wrapped his decaying tentacles tighter around the old fisherman. "Where did you put the strawberry cheesecake?"

As with the exclamation mark in the middle of a sentence in the previous chapter, this only works if used with dashes or ellipses or some other way of separating off the phrase. It would look highly odd if the question mark was swimming alone in the middle of the sentence.

NO QUESTION MARK

Sometimes you wrap a question into a statement:

> Gollum asked if anyone had seen his ring.

> The Cyberdyne System's model T-1000 Terminator pondered whether he should plant some daisies.

Although these sentences are about questions, they are not the actual questions coming from the characters' mouths. Therefore you don't need a question mark.

CHAPTER 9

Dash

I'll admit it: I love dashes. They are positively my favourite punctuation mark. Why? Because you can get seriously creative with them. They offer so many choices. And they look great.

On the other hand, teachers usually hate dashes, because you can use them for almost everything, thereby avoiding getting to grips with the other punctuation marks. Understandably, teachers often try to stop you using them. However: resist! Embrace dashes. Centuries ago, the great novelists used dashes everywhere. They festooned pages with them. You shouldn't go that far any more, but used well, dashes will add zip and sparkle to your writing.

WHAT DOES IT DO?

The dash has five main uses. (1) Super-strength comma. (2) Interrupted speech. (3) Lists, explanations, and expansions. (4) Speech. (5) Swear words and blanked out words.

SUPER-STRENGTH COMMA

A pair of dashes can act as a set of super-strength commas. Look at the following sentence:

> Han Solo, now truly frightened, gibbered as Jabba the Hut handed him the gold spandex underwear.

If we rewrite the sentence with dashes, it creates a different effect:

> Han Solo — now truly frightened — gibbered as Jabba the Hut handed him the gold spandex underwear.

The dashes here really lift the phrase "now truly frightened" out of the sentence and make it pop. The reader is left in absolutely no doubt that Han Solo is not in a good place.

INTERRUPTED SPEECH

In fiction, a dash can show that someone has been interrupted:

> "It's a Ridgeback," Harry gaped in wonder, "a kind of dragon with four — "

> "Oh, do *stop* mansplaining," Hermione rolled her eyes. "I can see what it is."

Some people use an ellipsis for this (see Chapter 14), but a dash is better.

LISTS, EXPLANATIONS, AND EXPANSIONS

As we've seen, colons can be used to introduce lists and explanations (see Chapter 5):

> All sorts of things get stuck in Wookie fur: duct tape, intergalactic dust, and small animals.

> Simba's secret was out: he hated her Chihuahua.

> Santa Claus wanted just one thing for Christmas: revenge.

We can rewrite these with dashes:

> All sorts of things get stuck in Wookie fur —
> duct tape, intergalactic dust, and small animals.

> Simba's secret was out — he hated her
> Chihuahua.

> Santa Claus wanted just one thing for Christmas
> — revenge.

A dash changes the look and feel of these sentences. It's subtle, but it makes the sentences more open and loose. More relaxed. You probably wouldn't use dashes like this in very formal or technical writing, but it's quite common in fiction.

SPEECH

You may sometimes see a dash being used to introduce direct speech, instead of quotation marks.

> Snow White could not believe her eyes.

> —That's my porridge, she snarled at the startled
> woodsman.

> She advanced on him, training the .50 cal directly
> at his spoon.

This was fashionable once, but it's less common now.

SWEAR WORDS AND BLANKED OUT WORDS

People also used to use dashes to blank out impolite words. You don't come across it so much any more, mainly because publishers are now happier to print swear words. But in the past you'd see:

> "Oh, f— it," Eeyore concluded, kicking over the honey pot.

These days you are more likely to see just one letter replaced with a dash:

> "Oh, f–ck it," Eeyore concluded, kicking over the honey pot.

"Oh, f— it," Eeyore concluded, kicking over the honey pot.

In some old-fashioned fiction, you would also see it if the writer was setting the story in a fictional place, or if they wanted a character to remain anonymous:

> The Transylvanian night was black and icy as Professor Von C-3PO's landspeeder drew into the ravaged village of G——.

> That fateful tea dance where Lord Voldemort met his love, Mrs M——, a gentle widow of mature years.

This use of the dash is not so common any more, but you'll still see it if you read older books.

EM DASH (—) AND EN DASH (–)

If you're interested in printing and layout, there are, technically speaking, two completely different dashes: em dashes and en dashes. Almost all modern word processors have both, but you may have to hunt for them.

Before we look at the difference between em and en dashes, a quick warning. Never use a hyphen (-) when you want a dash. Hyphens are a completely different punctuation mark (see the following chapter). Hyphens are only for compound words like co-defendant or good-looking.

The visual difference between hyphens, en dashes, and em dashes is in the length of the line. People don't really bother with a distinction when writing by hand, but there is a real difference in printed text:

hyphen	-
en dash	–
em dash	—

The em dash is the longest. It's twice the length of an en dash, and in the old days of printing it was as wide as the letter 'M' (hence the name, em dash). This is the dash you want ninety-nine per cent of the time. Traditionally, it's always used "closed", which means it doesn't have spaces either side of it:

> The minion—breathing heavily now—reached for the cotton wool.

The en dash is shorter. It's twice the length of a hyphen, and in the old days of printing it was as wide as the letter 'N' (hence the name, en dash). It's used between numbers, dates, times, and other numerical ranges. Traditionally it's also used closed, with no spaces either side of it:

> 1974–85
> pages 1–20
> 9.00 pm–10.00 pm

Just to confuse things, fashions change, and it's

becoming increasingly popular to use "open" en dashes (i.e., with spaces either side) instead of closed em dashes. Where you used to see this:

> Harry did not blink—not once—as he stuffed the last of the Blast-Ended Skrewt into the wood chipper.

You now increasingly see this:

> Harry did not blink – not once – as he stuffed the last of the Blast-Ended Skrewt into the wood chipper.

The difference is only really one of look and feel. Most readers probably wouldn't notice or care. But layout is a subtle art which sends messages to the reader about the kind of text they're reading. For that reason, a more serious book might still have closed em dashes, while a modern airport thriller might opt for open en dashes.

Just to prove my point that punctuation is creative and personal, in this book I have used yet another variation: open em dashes.

When all is said and done, you can use whichever dashes you want, and you can make them open or closed. As with most advice related to punctuation, just be consistent.

———◆———

CHAPTER 10

Hyphen

The hyphen should not be confused with the dash. The difference is simple but important. Hyphens go inside words. Dashes go between them (except when blanking out words, see the previous chapter).

WHAT DOES IT DO?

A hyphen has three uses. (1) Compound words. (2) Multi-word adjectives. (3) Word breaks.

COMPOUND WORDS

Some words have a short prefix like "co", "pre", "anti", "post", and so on. People used to write these with a hyphen:

    co-operate
    pre-cook
    anti-hero
    post-modern

These days not many people bother with the hyphen. They just write:

    cooperate
    precook
    antihero
    postmodern

Putting hyphens into these kinds of words now looks old-fashioned.

However, hyphens are still used in certain multipart words:

    build-up
    mother-in-law
    booby-trap

In these examples, the hyphen is part of the way the word is spelled. There is no simple way to know whether the word should be "booby trap", "boobytrap", or "booby-trap". With these multi-part words you need to reach for a dictionary to double-check you've got it right.

MULTI-WORD ADJECTIVES

If a number of words are being strung together to make a multi-word adjective, then it's normal to hyphenate them:

> its broccoli-smeared fangs
>
> the swipe-and-wipe guillotine
>
> Erik Bloodaxe's razor-sharp wit

An exception to this is that you don't put a hyphen if the first word ends in "-ly":

> A softly scented cyclops.

It's just one of those conventions.

WORD BREAKS

In traditional books, magazines, and newspapers, printers spent a lot of time fiddling with the gaps between letters and words. These were the dark arts of kerning and tracking. If they got to the end of a line and found they were mid-way through a word, their solution was to break the word and add a hyphen to show that the word had not finished:

> Thor hurled his hammer, Mjölnir, at the ad-
> vancing beavers.

Good dictionaries show you the places in words where
you are allowed to break them. For example:

> ad-vancing

This kind of hyphenation is less relevant today because
word processors automatically "justify" text so words
are never broken at the end of a line. However, most
word processors allow you to turn on hyphenation if
you want more professional letter spacing.

Thor hurled his hammer, Mjölnir, at the ad-
vancing beavers.

CHAPTER II

Apostrophe

The apostrophe is very simple, but it's the most abused punctuation mark of them all.

Some people might suggest that the way we use apostrophes is changing. But for now, in formal writing, you absolutely need to stick with traditional usage. Nothing screams "unreliable writer" more than basic apostrophe errors.

WHAT DOES IT DO?

The apostrophe has two uses. (1) Belonging. (2)

Missing letter.

BELONGING

An apostrophe shows that something belongs to someone or something.

> The unicorn's prize collection of mantraps.
>
> The dementor's retirement home.

In these examples, the apostrophe shows that the mantraps and the retirement home belong to the stated owner.

People get confused about this, but it's a pretty simple idea. You can show belonging in two ways:

> The yoga mat of Pontius Pilate.
>
> Pontius Pilate's yoga mat.

Both sentences mean exactly the same thing: the yoga mat belongs to Pontius Pilate. You can indicate this with the word "of" or with an apostrophe. The choice is yours.

Remember though, if there is more than one person, you have to put the apostrophe after the final "s":

The ghoulish monks' tasty tinctures.

The hobbits' nuclear facility.

Also remember that some words are singular, even though they are about more than one person:

The vampire children's favourite party game.

The Ostrogoth women's support network.

It's no more complicated than that.

MISSING LETTER

An apostrophe can also be used to show that a letter (or more than one letter) is missing. Look at the following abbreviations:

I'm, I'll, I've, I'd, you're, you'll, you've, you'd, she's, she'll, she'd, we're, we'll, we've, we'd, they're, they'll, they've, they'd, it's, it'll, doesn't, won't, can't, shouldn't, and so on

In each case, the apostrophe is standing in for one or more letters:

I'm	is short for	I am
you're	is short for	you are
she'd	is short for	she had or would
they're	is short for	they have

Using an apostrophe in these words is mostly straightforward, although there are some odd ones. For example:

shan't	is short for	shall not
won't	is short for	will not

There's no real logic to these words. They've evolved over time in an attempt to write down words the way people say them. If you're unsure about spelling them, you'll need to check in a dictionary. Several decades ago you were only really supposed to use these words when writing what someone was saying. Now you see these words in all sorts of contexts.

THE GREENGROCER'S APOSTROPHE

The commonest — and most criticized — apostrophe mistake is known as the "Greengrocer's Apostrophe". This name comes from the fact it was first noticed on signs written by greengrocers. It's now everywhere, and so widespread that maybe one day it'll become acceptable. For now, however, it's definitely not okay.

The Greengrocer's Apostrophe happens when someone tries to use an apostrophe to make a word plural:

fresh plum's	instead of	fresh plums
cold drink's	instead of	cold drinks
MP3's	instead of	MP3s

The rule is crystal clear and blindingly simple. NEVER EVER use an apostrophe to make anything plural. An apostrophe cannot make a plural. It just can't. Not ever. Never. Not once. Don't do it.

Well. Almost never. It might just be alright to use an apostrophe to make a number or letter plural:

The dodo packed her eggs into cartons of 12's.

The octopus took a pen in each tentacle and settled down to check he had dotted all the i's and crossed all the t's in his book report.

The dodo packed her eggs into cartons of 12s.

But even here I'd recommend you don't. People may think they're Greengrocer's Apostrophes. I'd use nothing for the number and quotation marks for the letters:

> The dodo packed her eggs into cartons of 12s.

> The octopus took a pen in each tentacle and settled down to check he had dotted all the "i"s and crossed all the "t"s in his book report.

When it comes to apostrophes, it's better to be safe than sorry.

ONE TO WATCH: ITS AND IT'S

This is actually very straightforward, and there's no need for confusion. As we have seen, apostrophes can show belonging:

> The vampire's dental floss.

Or they can indicate where something is missing:

> Don't scream.

It's usually pretty easy to know whether the apostrophe is for belonging or something missing. The only tricky one sometimes is the difference between "its" and "it's". Here, you just need to remember that the apostrophe is for the missing letter. It never indicates possession. "It's" always means "it is" or "it has". That's it.

> "It's your turn," Minnie said, attaching Mickey to the Special Forces issue parachute.
>
> The siren started with some warm-up scales.

While we're on the subject, remember there are no such words as "our's", "your's", or "their's". They don't exist.

"It's your turn," Minnie said, attaching Mickey to the Special Forces issue parachute.

FOR BLACK BELTS: NAMES ENDING IN S

Many people were taught at school that they must write:

Elvis' sandwich   not   Elvis's sandwich

In fact, both are correct.

For example, the *New King James Bible* says: Moses's. And in central London you'll find an area called St James's with a venerable gentlemen's club called Brooks's.

The best rule of thumb these days is that you should write it how you say it. Of course, people say things differently, so there will be variations. But, in principle, think about how the reader would say the word if reading aloud:

Jar Jar Binks's enhanced theory of relativity.

Moses's Stone Age tablet.

King Charles's spaniel.

There is one traditional exception, although you're not likely to use it very often. In books about theology, traditional printers write Jesus' and not Jesus's.

CHAPTER 12

Quotation Mark

These are called quotation marks, quotes, inverted commas, or speech marks.

There are two types: singles (' ') and doubles (" "). You can use either. There are no strict rules. In practice, single quotation marks are more common in England, where printers traditionally like a lighter, cleaner look to the page. Double quotation marks are more common in the U.S. One benefit of double quotation marks is that they avoid confusion with apostrophes.

Use whichever you prefer, but be consistent in any

single piece of writing. Use one or the other. Not both.

WHAT DOES IT DO?

Quotation marks have three uses. (1) Direct speech. (2) Quotations and references. (3) "Air quotes".

DIRECT SPEECH

Quotation marks show that someone is speaking:

> "Hello," Dracula chirped.

> 'Now, you die,' Kermit grimaced.

It's very straightforward, but remember to add the comma (see Chapter 4).

QUOTATIONS AND REFERENCES

You can also use quotation marks when you're quoting something or referring to it:

> The wraith stared numbly at the word 'Ghostbusters' emblazoned on the man's overalls.

If you're using quotation marks inside another set of quotation marks, then switch to the ones you haven't already used:

> "I was very clear in my memo," Cthulhu
> thundered. "I said 'no bullying the prawns'."

In other words, put singles inside doubles and doubles inside singles.

"I was very clear in my memo," Cthulhu thundered. "I said 'no bullying the prawns'."

"AIR QUOTES"

Sometimes you might want to highlight that a word is being used sarcastically, ironically, or incorrectly. If you were speaking, you might do air quotes with your fingers:

The amoeba had heard enough of Darwin and his
so-called "theories" of evolution.

Again, you can use single or double quotation marks
for air quotes.

HOW TO PUNCTUATE SPEECH

People sometimes struggle with how to punctuate
speech. It's actually very easy.

If you're using the "she said", "he explained", "she
rasped", "he purred" structure, you just use a comma
and keep it all in the same sentence:

> "No, oh God, not the doilies," he begged the
> advancing manatee.

The same principle applies if you're just breaking up
the spoken sentence:

> "Jedi good will you not make … ," Yoda
> lamented, "fashion sense have you none."

If the speaker ends a sentence and starts a new one,
then you should, too:

> "Okay, settle down," he ordered the class. "Write
> me a thousand words on the history of the string
> vest."

If you don't want to explain how the person said the words, then don't. Use a period (or question mark or exclamation mark) to finish his or her speech, then carry on with the next bit of action.

> "Armour-piercing, you say?" Rapunzel eyed the belt of bullets appreciatively.

> "I'll be back." The Terminator left his bride standing at the altar as he headed for the biker bar.

If you're in any doubt, just pick up a couple of novels and see how it's done. You'll find it's very straightforward.

CHAPTER 13

Brackets

In the UK they are called brackets. In the U.S. they're parentheses. There is also some variation in names for other, more technical, members of the bracket family. In British English [ ] are called square brackets and { } are curly brackets, whereas they are brackets and braces in U.S. English. In this chapter we're mainly concerned with brackets/parentheses. I'm going to call them brackets.

My best advice with brackets is to avoid them as much as possible in normal writing. They're irritating, and if they crop up too often they drive readers mad. In most cases you can simply replace them with commas or dashes.

WHAT DOES IT DO?

Brackets have one main use: to add non-essential or extra information.

EXAMPLES

Brackets can be used to drop in information that is outside the flow of the sentence:

> The Tusken Raiders (sometimes called Sand People) wondered how they would get the banthas onto the flight to Las Vegas.

The brackets here show that the words inside them don't really have anything to do with the main flow of the sentence. You can remove the brackets and the words between them without damaging the meaning of the sentence. They're really just there to add a little shot of extra information.

But brackets are annoying because they interrupt the sentence, and in many cases you can simply remove them. The following two ways of writing the sentence work just as well:

The Tusken Raiders, sometimes called Sand People, wondered how they would get the banthas onto the flight to Las Vegas.

The Tusken Raiders — sometimes called Sand People — wondered how they would get the banthas onto the flight to Las Vegas.

That said, there are times when you really do need brackets, usually to add essential information in more formal or technical writing:

To assemble the guillotine, insert the upright case (Part A) into the long bench (Part B), then slot in the slanted blade (Part C). As always when working in your home workshop, watch your fingers. When completed, keep safely away from children and aristocrats.

The insane Countess Bathory (1560–1614) loved a good blood bath.

In these instances, using brackets allows you to add vital information without destroying the sentence too much. Keep brackets for this kind of use. Try and ditch them everywhere else.

The Tusken Raiders, sometimes called Sand People, wondered how they would get the banthas onto the flight to Las Vegas.

OTHER BRACKETS

Other members of the bracket family have more technical uses. Square brackets are usually used to show words that were added by someone other than the writer, normally to clarify the sense:

> The Ewok decided to keep it [the mankini] for dressing up.

Curly brackets are mainly used as specialist symbols in science, mathematics, coding, and technical literature.

The Ewok decided to keep it [the mankini] for dressing up.

CHAPTER 14

Ellipsis

The ellipsis is incredibly straightforward. Sometimes people don't realize it's a punctuation mark, but it is, and it has specific uses.

Ellipses look best "open", with a space either side:

> "I came, I saw ... I wondered why I bothered."

> Cthulhu looked numbly at the plate of seafood linguine. "What on earth ... ?"

WHAT DOES IT DO?

The ellipsis has three uses. (1) Missing words. (2) Pause. (3) Trailing off.

MISSING WORDS

In formal writing, an ellipsis shows that you've chopped out some words. If you take the *Bleak House* quotation in Chapter 6 and cut some of it out, you'd use an ellipsis to show where text has been removed:

> Harold Skimpole loves to see the sun shine; loves to hear the wind blow … loves to hear the birds, those choristers in Nature's great cathedral.

This type of ellipsis is an act of politeness to the reader, giving them a heads-up that the original text has been shortened.

PAUSE

Another use of the ellipsis, usually in fiction, is to create a pause, often when someone is thinking:

> "I'd like the … quinoa risotto," the zombie announced, pulling out his omnitool.

The ellipsis here just adds a bit of space, and makes the speech seem more natural.

TRAILING OFF

You can also use an ellipsis when a character's thoughts trail off. Exactly like when someone says, "dot dot dot":

> The werewolf looked at the meaty opera singer. He did so want to hear him sing 'Nessun dorma', but it was well past his lunch time …

> "Constant vigilance …" Barty Crouch mumbled as he fell asleep.

This type of ellipsis is much more common in fiction.

CHAPTER 15

Two Punctuation Marks

Sometimes you might find you have two punctuation marks next to each other. This can raise questions about whether it's necessary to keep both, or what order they should be in.

TWO PERIODS

You may find you have two periods next to each other. For example:

> It was already 11.59 p.m.. He would be going furry soon.

In practice, I wouldn't put periods in "p.m." (see Chapter 3), but I have done here for the sake of the example. The rule is simple. Don't double up. Delete one of them:

> It was already 11.59 p.m. He would be going
> furry soon.

This is really part of the fashion for minimalism. It's always best to use the fewest number of punctuation marks to get the job done.

PERIOD AND SOMETHING ELSE

You may find you have a period and a different punctuation mark. In this case, you keep both:

> Was it already 12.10 a.m.? Where was the fur?

This is okay, because you're not repeating the same punctuation mark, and it wouldn't make sense if you deleted one of them.

QUOTATION MARK
AND SOMETHING ELSE

You quite often have a quotation mark next to another punctuation mark.

Quotation Mark and Period or Comma

You most often have a period or comma next to a quotation mark. The tricky question that arises is: what order do you put them in?

In the U.S., it's accepted that you put the punctuation mark inside the quotation mark:

> "Not again," the witch muttered grumpily, realizing she had left her favourite newt at the chiropodist.

The alternative, which you will also see, is to put the punctuation mark outside the quotation mark, like this:

> "The secret to effective curses", the witch scribbled, "is good oral hygiene."

> The Elephant's Child decided to stop asking everyone "what", "how", "why", and other questions that always resulted in physical injury.

The logic behind the comma outside the quotation mark in the witch curse example above is that the witch did not write a comma in her original sentence after the word "curses", so we should not put one there. Instead, placing it outside the quotation mark shows it's the writer's comma not the witch's. (And you'll see I put a comma after the quotation mark in the previous sentence for exactly the same reason.)

U.S. publishers are pretty consistent in their approach. UK publishers less so. Style guides sometimes set out complex rules. If the choice is yours, my recommendation is that the U.S. system of putting the comma inside the quotation mark is simple, logical, and always looks neat with normal dialogue. For more technical purposes like the two examples above, you may want to put the comma outside the quotation mark, but use your judgment and go with whatever seems most logical and clear.

Quotation Mark and Question or Exclamation Mark

You may need to put a question mark or exclamation mark alongside a quotation mark.

Here the best guidance is to do whatever makes sense for the sentence.

For example, in the following sentence, the frog is asking the question, so the question mark should go inside the quotation mark along with what the frog is saying:

The frog looked up anxiously, "Will it hurt?"

By contrast, in the following sentence, the bodysnatcher is asking the question, so the question mark should go outside the quotation mark:

The bodysnatcher wondered if he had heard right. Had the vampire just said, "Make my day"?

It's all a question of context. Use your judgement.

The bodysnatcher wondered if he had heard right. Had the vampire just said, "Make my day"?

Quotation Mark and Brackets

With brackets, it's a bit more obvious what to do.

There are two possibilities: a set of brackets nested inside a sentence, or a whole sentence in brackets.

In the first case you keep the punctuation outside the brackets:

> The dark rider galloped off into the night
> (unaware of the GPS tracker in his lunchbox).

This is logical. The brackets are inside the sentence, so you put the period at the very end of the sentence as normal.

On the other hand, if the whole sentence is in brackets, then it makes sense to put the period inside the brackets:

> Cinderella threw the shoe at him. (She'd always
> hated princes.) It arced through the air, its
> sharpened heel aimed straight at his bald patch.

This is also logical. The whole sentence is an aside, therefore the words and punctuation go inside the brackets.

CHAPTER 16

Numbers

Although numbers are not punctuation marks, writing them correctly creates an excellent impression, and shows you know what you're doing.

IN FICTION

Write out numbers in full, in words:

> Little Red Riding Hood buried eight wolves that day.

You need to be a bit sensible with this, though.

Sometimes it's just silly to write numbers as words. For example:

> He was ninety-nine point nine nine nine per cent certain that the Wookie just stroked his leg.

You'd almost certainly make it simpler for the reader and write:

> He was 99.999 per cent certain that the Wookie just stroked his leg.

IN TECHNICAL WRITING

In more technical forms of writing, you can use figures like 23 or 47. However, there's a very widespread convention that if you're going to do this, you write one to nine as words, then use figures for 10 and above:

> Prince Charming gagged at the sight of the five moss-covered toenails.

> Cinderella carefully arranged the 18 fragmentation grenades.

If you do this, it can sometimes look a little odd if you have numbers under 10 and over 10 in the same sentence, but it's just how it's done:

> Little Red Riding ducked as the two jets and 14 helicopters screamed overhead.

Anyone who knows about writing will be aware that you have written this correctly. Of course, you are under no obligation to write numbers like this, but be aware that lots of people do, and it looks professional.

HYPHENATE

When you write numbers out as full words, you need to use hyphens in certain cases. The rule is that you hyphenate numbers between twenty-one and ninety-nine:

> Twenty-three neurotic elves.
>
> Forty-seven elated dementors.

But note that you don't use hyphens with hundreds, thousands, millions, etc.:

> One hundred and thirty-seven and a half zombies emerged, unaccustomedly relaxed, from the massage parlour.
>
> Three thousand and sixty-two rabid minions.

Once you start doing this, you'll see it's easy and straightforward, and it looks very smart.

CHAPTER 17

-IZE or -ISE

T his chapter is not strictly about punctuation, but the question of whether to use "-ize" or "-ise" often causes confusion, so it's worth explaining.

GENERAL PRINCIPLES

You sometimes hear people today — especially in the UK — say that using a "z" in words like "organize" or "specialization" is a modern American innovation, and that an "s" is the correct English spelling.

In fact, the opposite is true. The "z" spelling is very old, and has been used in Britain since medieval times.

The reason our ancestors chose "-ize" is that it comes from the ancient Greek ending *-izein*, which has the Greek letter "zeta", which is a "z" in English.

Because of this origin, the "ize" spelling has always been standard in English, and used down the centuries by many of Britain's best-known writers:

Richard of Gloucester (d. 1200)
William Langland (d. 1386)
Geoffrey Chaucer (d. 1400)
King James Bible (1611)
William Shakespeare (d. 1616)
John Donne (d. 1631)
John Milton (d. 1674)
Dr Samuel Johnson (d. 1784)
Jane Austen (d. 1817)
Walter Scott (d. 1832)
Samuel Taylor Coleridge (d. 1834)
Charles Dickens (d. 1870)
Thomas Carlyle (d. 1881)
Charles Darwin (d. 1882)
Thomas Hardy (d. 1928)
Arthur Conan Doyle (d. 1930)

James Joyce (d. 1941)
George Orwell (d. 1950)
Winston Churchill (d. 1965)
J R R Tolkein (d. 1973)
Agatha Christie (d. 1976)
… the list could be many times longer.

Using "-ise" as an alternative form only dates from the mid-1700s, when some people wanted to make English look more fashionable by copying French spelling, in which "-ise" is normal.

In the U.S., the traditional "z" spelling remained widespread, and became standard when Noah Webster's *American Dictionary of the English Language* used it throughout in 1828.

Today in Britain, many publishers, universities, academic journals, and encyclopaedias continue to use "-ize", as they always have done. The *Oxford English Dictionary*, which is the bible of British English spelling, firmly favours "-ize", and as a result it's sometimes known as Oxford Spelling.

WHEN "-ISE" IS COMPULSORY

To complicate matters a little, in both U.S. and British

English, there are several words that have to be spelled "-ise". This is because they don't come from the *-izein* Greek root. They include:

> advertise, advise, apprise, chastise, comprise, compromise, despise, devise, disguise, excise, exercise, improvise, incise, prise, promise, revise, supervise, surmise, surprise, televise

Unless you're an expert in etymology, you simply have to learn these. Some people find that a pain, which is why "-ise" has become so popular, as you can use it each and every time without exceptions! When *The Times* newspaper in London switched from "-ize" to "-ise" in 1992, it gave this simplicity as the reason.

WHICH?

These days, "-ize" and "-ise" are both completely acceptable. Both are widespread. You can use either, and it's a free choice. (This book uses "-ize".) Neither is more correct than the other, although "-ize" is a little more traditional and etymologically accurate. As always, just be consistent in any single piece of writing.

CHAPTER 18

U.S. English and British English — It's the Same

It's easy to get excited about the different names we use for "periods", "full stops", "parentheses", "brackets", and a few other punctuation marks in the U.S. and Britain.

However, when it comes to good punctuation style in American and British English, there is no significant difference.

There are only two places in this book where I mention small variations between U.S. and British practice.

One is a U.S. printing tradition for a comma and a quotation mark next to each other. This will be of interest to people writing stories.

The other is a specific circumstance in which some U.S. publishers like a capital letter after a colon. It's pretty specialized, and unlikely to be relevant to most people.

That's it. Don't let differences like variations in names and spellings fool you. When it comes to sound punctuation, American and British English are identical.

CHAPTER 19

For Black Belts

The following words do not appear (much) in this book, but you will find them used extensively in more traditional punctuation and grammar books.

Words in bold are defined in the list.

Adjective　　　Gives descriptive detail about a **noun**:

　　　　　　　　the *disgruntled* Orc

　　　　　　　　the *stampeding* scorpions

Adverb　　　Gives descriptive detail about a **verb, adjective**, or another **adverb**:

　　　　　　　　He sneezed *demonically*.
　　　　　　　　(describing the verb "sneezed")

　　　　　　　　The *unfeasibly* eloquent Wookie.
　　　　　　　　(describing the adjective "eloquent")

　　　　　　　　The elf felt seasick as he disapparated *too* swiftly.
　　　　　　　　(describing the adverb "swiftly")

Clause

A unit within a sentence that contains a **verb**. The two common types are (1) main clauses and (2) subordinate clauses. Subordinate clauses can be either (a) relative clauses or (b) conditional claus-es.

(1) Main clauses. These have at least a **subject** and a **verb**, and can therefore stand by themselves as a sentence, if you want them to:

> *the hobbit desperately tried the Manolo Blahniks,* but his feet were too long.

(2) Subordinate clauses. These only make sense when combined with a main clause:

> *After living 60 years in the Shire,* Frodo yearned for the mean streets of the ghetto.

(a) Relative clauses. These are usually introduced by "who", "which", or "that":

> The elf *who collects grenade launchers*.

> Gimli, *who was still feeling groggy,* trod on his axe.

> The ancient sepulchre, *which lay open*, could be hired for parties.

> The bastard sword *that Tigger wanted for his birthday*.

(b) Conditional clauses. These usually begin with "if" or "unless" and are about something that is possible or probable:

> *If they hope to make it to Mount Doom*, they'll need to stay hydrated.

> *Unless we stop him by dawn*, he'll drone on for all eternity.

Conjunction   Connects words, phrases, or
clauses:

> *and, because, but, if,* etc.

Noun   A word for people, things, places,
or ideas. A naming word. You
can put "a" or "the" in front of
a noun:

> the *goblin*
> a *zombie*

Names of places, people, and
organizations are called proper
nouns. You cannot put "'a" or
"the" in front of a proper noun:

> *Dracula*
> *Transylvania*

Object
The bit of the sentence or phrase that usually comes after the **verb**. There are two types: (1) direct object and (2) indirect object.

(1) Direct object. These are what the **verb's** action affects:

> The monk brought along a *trebuchet*.

> The druid traded in *his cauldron* for an espresso machine.

(2) Indirect object. Usually a person, animal, or thing that is affected by the direct object:

> The hippogryph gave *him* the ride of a lifetime.

> He owed *the dementor* a back rub.

Pronoun

A special type of **noun** that stands for the **noun**:

I, you, she, him, it, they, etc.

Subject

A **noun** or **pronoun** that the sentence or clause is about:

The *Balrog* gazed longingly at the bubbly, foamy bath.

Maximinus Thrax gargled voraciously.

Verb

A "doing" word that explains what the **subject** is doing, has done, or will do:

The Venus Flytrap *rustled* its leaves threateningly.

The octopus *was* the star of the typing pool.

The octopus was the star of the typing pool.

Quotations
and Acknowledgements

Epigraph

The quotation from Mark Twain appears in Mark Twain, *A Connecticut Yankee in King Arthur's Court*, Bernard Stein (ed.), *The Works of Mark Twain*, Berkeley, University of California Press, 1979, vol. 9, p. 582.

Epigraph

The quotation from Lord Byron appears in Peter Cochrane, *Manfred: an Edition of Byron's Manuscripts and a Collection of Essays*, Newcastle upon Tyne, Cambridge Scholars Publishing, 2015, p. 29.

Epigraph

The quotation from Charlotte Brontë (written under her pseudonym of C Bell) appears in Charlotte Brontë *Selected Letters of Charlotte Brontë*, Margaret Smith (ed.), Oxford, Oxford University Press, 2007, letter 54, p. 87.

Chapter 1

The Shakespeare quotation is taken from Act 3, Scene
1 of *Hamlet* as it appears in the Bodleian First Folio,
which is listed in the Bodleian's catalogue as *Mr.
William Shakespeares comedies, histories, & tragedies. : Published
according to the true originall copies..*, Isaac Iaggard and Ed.
Blount, London, 1623, p. 265. If you really want the
original spelling, layout, and punctuation, here it is:

> To be, or not to be, that is the Queſtion :
> Whether 'tis Nobler in the minde to ſuffer
> The Slings and Arrowes of outrageous Fortune,'
> Or to take Armes againſt a Sea of troubles,
> And by oppoſing end them : to dye, to ſleepe
> No more ; and by a ſleepe, to ſay we end
> The Heart-ake, and the thouſand Naturall
>   ſhockes
> That Fleſh is heyre too?

Chapter 1

The quotation from 1762 is from Robert Lowth, *A
Short Introduction to English Grammar: with Critical Notes*,
London, A Millar (publisher), J Hughs (printer), 1762.
I haven't managed to check a copy of the original
1762 edition, but the quotation appears on p. 141 of
the 1771 edition (London, J Dodsley in Pall-mall and
T Cadell in the Strand). Lowth was a bishop and had
been an Oxford professor of poetry. The book was

immensely popular, published around forty-five times between 1762 and 1800.

Chapter 7

The quotation from George Orwell about his novel *Coming Up for Air* (London, Victor Gollancz, 1939) appears in George Orwell, *The Complete Works of George Orwell*, P Davison (ed.), London, Secker and Warburg, 1998, vol. 7, pp. 249–50.

Chapter 7

The quotation from Kurt Vonnegut appears in Kurt Vonnegut, *A Man Without a Country*, New York, Seven Sisters Press, 2005, p. 23.

Chapter 10

The quotation from F Scott Fitzgerald appears in Sheilah Graham, *Beloved Infidel. The Education of a Woman*, New York, Henry Holt and Co., 1958, pp. 197–8.